ABSOLUTE TRUTH WILL SET US *Free!*

ABSOLUTE TRUTH WILL SET US *Free!*

(How marginalized people were impacted when a triple murder occurred in 1939 that caused the destruction of the innocent and how it applies even today in 2024. Unfortunately, some things have never changed)

DRUANNE (DRU) CARPENTER EARLL, M.ED., ED.S.

(The paternal granddaughter of Floyd Franklin Carpenter, Sr.)

PALMETTO
PUBLISHING
Charleston, SC
www.PalmettoPublishing.com

Copyright © 2024 by DruAnne (Dru) Carpenter Earll

All rights reserved
No portion of this book may be reproduced, stored in a retrieval system, or transmitted in any form by any means–electronic, mechanical, photocopy, recording, or other–except for brief quotations in printed reviews, without prior permission of the author.

First Edition

Paperback: 979-8-8229-3706-2
eBook: 979-8-8229-3707-9

A true story of the tragic injustices and destruction of two marginalized families in the 1939 triple murder case, W.D. Lyons v. Oklahoma, and how this system continues to cause injustice and destruction.

Two Convicts Held in State Triple Slaying

Farmer Says Trusties Made Him Drive Them To Victims' Home

FORT TOWSON, Jan. 12.—(Special.)—Solution of the gruesome triple arson tragedy here New Year's eve, when Mr. and Mrs. Elmer Rogers and their 4-year-old son, Elvie Dean, died in their burning home, was claimed Friday by Roy Harmon, Choctaw county sheriff.

Behind prison walls at McAlester Friday were two convicts from the Sawyer prison camp near here, both accused of the triple murder by Houston Lambert, 28 years old, Fort Towson farmer.

Drove Pair to Scene

Lambert told county officers early Friday morning that the two prison camp trusties, at the point of a gun, forced him to drive them to the Rogers home the night of the tragedy.

"They threatened to kill me if I said anything," Lambert told Sheriff Harmon in explaining why he had concealed his knowledge of the crime for nearly two weeks.

Camp Official Ousted

As the death story unfolded, Jess Dunn, warden of the penitentiary at McAlester, fired the first shot in a prison camp cleanup at Fort Towson. He announced discharge of Joe Adair, sergeant at the camp, because he gave the convicts "too much freedom." Dunn appointed Carl Dunlap, a veteran prison employe, to succeed Adair.

At McAlester early Friday, Lambert confronted the suspects in their cells and identified them as the two he drove to the Rogers home. Both convicts denied his statement.

One of the suspects, an Oklahoma City man, killed his bride of three weeks in 1926, then turned a gun on himself. He recovered from his wound and was convicted on a murder charge. He has served 14 years. The other suspect is serving a three-year term for burglary from Johnson county.

One Named by Fellow Convict

Two days after the Rogers home burned a trusty at the Stringtown sub-prison wrote a name on a piece of paper and handed it to prison officials after saying to another convict: "When that killing is solved that will be the man who did it."

The name on the paper was that of one of the men now suspected. This phase of the case was investigated by state officers and it was on their findings that Governor Phillips based his statement that he believed the implication of the convict by the prisoner was a "hoax."

One Nabbed Soon After Deaths

One of the two suspects, arrested immediately following the triple deaths, already was at McAlester prison, having been taken there to avoid possible violence. The second suspect, arrested Friday morning, was taken there immediately.

"I could smell liquor on their breath," Lambert continued. "I had seen them only once before and hardly knew them. They made me take my mother-in-law's car and drive them out to the Rogers home.

"They told me to stop about a quarter of a mile away. They left me after saying they would kill me if I didn't wait for them. After a while they came back and ordered me to take them back to the prison camp. I drove them back and as they got out of the car they again warned me they would kill me if I ever said anything about the trip."

One of the two men, a cook at the prison camp, who had the privileges of a trusty, was detained by Hugo county authorities immediately after the tragedy. Norman Horton, Choctaw county attorney said he had found out the cook had been writing to a Fort Towson woman, also that he was acquainted with Mrs. Rogers.

The suspect staunchly denied any knowledge of the three deaths, declared he was sober that night and had attended church services. Investigators from Governor Phillips office also reported to the executive that the suspect apparently had a clean bill despite Horton's protest that he could find no evidence of church services having been conducted near there.

Woman Gives Tip

The cook has been in the penitentiary at McAlester since his detention. The second suspect was taken to the prison from Fort Towson and delivered to the state prison at 3 a. m. Friday by Sheriff Harmon.

After seeking vainly for a "break" in the case, Choctaw county officials were told Thursday night by Mrs. Pruda May Wortz, 72 years old, Hugo, that her nephew, Lambert, could name the guilty persons.

Confronted with his aunt's statement Lambert told his story. Previously he had hinted to his aunt that he knew who committed the crime.

Two Children Escape

The charred bodies of the slain family were found in the ruins of their modest three-room farm home. Examination disclosed buckshot in the parent's bodies, indicating, authorities said, that they had been shot down before the home was fired. The child apparently died of suffocation and flames.

Get Cold Distress before it gets you!

Kalic Capsules

OKLAHOMA CITY TIMES

Paid Circulation Greater Than Any Other Evening Newspaper Published in Oklahoma

Evening, except Sunday. | TWENTY-EIGHT PAGES—500 N. BROADWAY, OKLAHOMA CITY, FRIDAY, JANUARY 12, 1940 | FINAL HOME EDITION | PRICE: FIVE CENTS

Landing on Frozen River Saves Airliner

Damaged in a forced landing, a disabled United Airlines plane is shown Friday on the ice in Rock river near Moline, Ill. (Wirephoto.)

Two Convicts Held in State Triple Slaying

Farmer Says Trusties Made Him Drive Them To Victims' Home

FORT TOWSON, Jan. 12.—(Special.)—Solution of the gruesome triple arson tragedy here New Year's eve, when Mr. and Mrs. Elmer Rogers and their 4-year-old son, Elvie Dean, died in their burning home, was claimed Friday by Ray Harmon, Choctaw county sheriff.

Behind prison walls at McAlester Friday were two convicts from the Sawyer prison camp near here, both accused in the triple murder by Houston Lambert, 28 years old, Fort Towson farmer.

Return of Chilton To State Refused By Ohio Governor

Said Governor Bricker:

Governor Bricker

Replied Governor Phillips:

Governor Phillips

'Good Conduct' Of Fugitive Praised By Bricker; Oklahoma Loses Second Time

COLUMBUS, Ohio, Jan. 12.—(AP)—Gov. John W. Bricker refused Friday to authorize the extradition to Oklahoma of Carlton B. Chilton, 44-year-old Cleveland man, who "made good" after escaping from an Oklahoma reformatory in 1917.

Roosevelt Asks Both Parties To Join in Planning Finn Help

Assistance Program Is Not Formulated Yet, Chief Says in Urging Nonpartisan Effort

PARIS, Jan. 12.—(AP)—Spain, Italy and southeastern European countries are shipping war materials to embattled Finland through France, an official spokesman said Friday. "The materials from these countries is considerable," he said, adding that volunteers also are en route from them to join the Finnish forces.

WASHINGTON, Jan. 12.—(AP)—President Roosevelt said Friday he had asked congressional leaders of both parties to work out the problem of giving assistance to Finland, but at the capitol slow progress was reported toward a solution.

Memo for the Reader:

Let's nominate a few heroes and heroines:

Eight Escape Death After Motor Fails Over Iowa City

Nazis Continue British Raids

Planes Are Driven Off By Anti-Aircraft Fire

Russians Launch New Drive in North

Mud at Northeast Highschool Is Here to Stay, Officials Fear

Law Prohibits Use of City, School Funds For Paving, and Property Owners Refuse to Pay

Aid Promised For Dam Job

Stephens Says City Will Get Funds From U. S.

With Emotion

VOLUME 48, NO. 274

SHERIFF REVEALS NEW EVIDENCE IN ROGERS SLAYINGS

Convicts At Prison Camp Are Identified With Fort Towson Case

FORT TOWSON, Okla., Jan. 12 — (AP) — A Sawyer, Okla., farmer identified two prison camp convicts today, Sheriff Roy Harmon said, as the New Year's eve slayers of Mr. and Mrs. Elmer Rogers and their 4-year-old son, Dean.

Harmon said the farmer, Houston Lambert, 28, signed a statement that the convicts, Frank Wellman and Floyd Carpenter, held him up and forced him to drive them to the Rogers home.

While he waited outside in the car, the farmer's statement continued, the convicts went into the house and two shots were fired. Then the frame dwelling burst into flames.

Exonerated By Warden

Wellman, serving a 30-year term for the murder of his bride in 1926, was arrested for questioning in the case 10 days ago but he was exonerated by Warden Jess Dunn, who said his inquiry indicated the convict was attending church services at the time of the slayings.

Governor Leon Phillips said a state investigation convinced him Wellman "didn't have a thing to do with it."

Carpenter, 33, is serving a three-year term for burglary from Johnston county. He had previously served another term for the same offense.

Earlier this morning Lambert was taken to the penitentiary at McAlester and confronted Wellman and Carpenter in their cells. Warden Dunn said he quickly identified them. Both convicts denied his statement.

Immediately after the interview, Dunn announced he had discharged Joe Adair, sergeant at the Fort Towson prison camp, because he gave the convicts "too much freedom." He appointed Carl Dunlap, a veteran prison employe, to replace him.

The 25 prisoners at the camp were hurried inside the prison walls and the warden said he would make a thorough investigation of previous conditions there.

James Glenn Rogers, 8, fled from his burning home, carrying his baby brother, Billy Don, and told officers two strangers shot his parents, then set fire to the dwelling.

---

was committed.

Officer Says Triple Slaying Still Unsolved

FORT TOWSON, Okla., Jan. 13 (AP)—The Fort Towson New Year's eve triple slaying appeared farther from solution tonight as one of the governor's special investigators declared a farmer informant had given three varying accounts of the crime.

Vern Cheatwood, one of two agents sent by Governor Phillips to probe the mystery, asserted that Houston Lambert, 28-year-old Sawyer farmer, was "making a different statement every day."

County officers had disclosed that Lambert signed a statement implicating three convicts of a nearby prison camp in the deaths of Mr. and Mrs. Elmer Rogers and their four-year-old son.

The farmer, who remained silent for two weeks, told county authorities yesterday the convicts forced him to drive them to the Rogers' three-room dwelling where they shot Mr. and Mrs. Rogers and fired the house.

Two of the convicts were identified by Lambert as Frank Wellman, serving 30 years for slaying his bride, and Floyd Carpenter, convicted of burglary.

HARRIS BOUND OVER TO TERM OF DISTRICT COURT

John Harris, charged with the theft of meat and lard from the smokehouse of Mrs. Bob Robertson and wearing apparel from the residence of Brice Woody of the Gillespie ranch, was bound over to the district court following his preliminary hearing, Saturday before Justice of the Peace Charley Ratliff.

Floyd Carpenter, charged with the same offense, preliminary trial was held Tuesday, and he also was bound over to the district court. Bond was set by the Justice at $1500 for each of the two men.

Woodmen Circle News

VERDICTS OF GUILTY MARK DIST. COURT

Walker Gets 3 Years; Rabb Guilty; Gibson One Year

District court criminal docket with Judge J. I. Goins presiding, closed here Tuesday afternoon after most of the defendants had either pleaded guilty or were found guilty by juries.

Johnny Raab, farm youth charged with manslaughter in connection with the death on December 16 of Clough Wester was found guilty by a jury after the members deliberated from Friday night until late Saturday afternoon. County Attorney W. D. French introduced witnesses to prove that Raab was driving recklessly at the time the accident occurred, in which Wester was killed. Raab will be sentenced by Judge Goins Tuesday.

In the case of Lee Walker and L. C. Privett, charged with grand larceny, the defense asked for severance and the state elected to try Walker. He was found guilty and sentenced to three years in the state penitentiary. The case was continued as to Privett.

John Harris and Floyd Carpenter pleaded guilty to four charges of burglary and was sentenced three years, to run concurrently, in two cases and two years each, to run concurrently, on the other charges, making a total of five years to be served.

Orville Dunn, husband of Nellie Kimes Dunn, sister of the notor-

Dedication

To the beautiful people in the world, (this means *you*, my friends), the ones who are not given full equality and civil rights, along with the respect and care that "the chosen" ones in society are given. Remember the great advocates and their heartfelt words of love and freedom: Thurgood Marshall, Dr. Martin Luther King Jr., Ruby Bridges, Mahatma Ghandi, Dalai Lama, Maya Angelou, Rosa Parks, Sylvia Rivera, Sally Ride, Hulleah Tsinhnahjinnie, Celia Chung, Marsha P. Johnson, Harvey Milk, RuPaul Charles, Joan Baez, Sofie Cruz, Sylvia Mendes, Elizabeth Stanton, Sojourner Truth, Susan B. Anthony, Frank James, Susan Shown Harjo, and the many other *countless, heroic activists* who have spent their lives and energies advocating for those of diversity so that we are *all* allowed genuine equal, civil rights!

dru

Acknowledgment

To my amazing and loving wife, Kimberly (Kim) Routliffe-Haybecker, thank you for filling that void in my heart that I have felt since the beginning of time and thank you for teaching me how to truly and comfortably "be me". I feel as though I am finally WHOLE! Your love, acceptance, and honesty keeps me curious, silly, and ever hopeful, always waiting for the next exciting adventure just around the corner! You have truly made me a better human being in this tricky world! I love you dearly, Kimmy, and I thank you!

To my sisters, Adele Montgomery, and Cindy Zeluff. Hey! Thanks for letting me test all my genius ideas and practices on you two as kids! I mean, some worked, and clearly, some didn't. (Okay, mistakes were clearly made, and I apologize.) But we played outside, interacted with cousins and friends, lived freely, and became awesome people! I love you both, and I hold you dear to my heart!

To my amazing triplets, Madison Earll, Andrew Earll, and Stephanie Earll-Baca, (in birth order and yes, Steph is *still* the baby by 30 seconds, guys.) I have truly been blessed by your arrival into this world. You each hold such individual and amazing strengths, laughter, and wonders within. Your skills are unique, your intuitions high, and your humor is dark, just like mine, but second to none! Feel confident to hold your truths and walk through this maze that we call life, with confidence and flare! It is a joy to be your mom, and remember, I have every faith in the world that each of you can hold this world in your hand and know that it is, indeed, your oyster! Thanks for your support throughout the years and always know that I love you guys more than I can ever express!

To Jake Haybecker and Lindsey Law: Stay strong and stay TRUE! Your skills are wonderful, and your laughter contagious! I thank both of you for the support that you show Kim and I. I love you guys! Kiss Dot and tell her that she's a great little lady, with the longest eyelashes that I have EVER seen!

To Ser Oliver~Newton and Lady Kya~Kitten, I love you two little rascally pup-Yorkies! It will be your turn finally! We shall write children's books and you two shall be the heroes that you are. I love you two!

To: ALL the beautiful people in this world past, present, and future, who dream, love, care, dare, and try. Those who long for justice, equality, truth, and peace in this world. Stand tall, be confident, and peacefully demand change and freedom! Save Mother Earth! Power to the People!

Notes to self- Hey Drubie...You did it! NICE!

That's me, on the right, with my beautiful wife, Kim on the left!

When-Then-We Cry

When a black teen goes out on a date in their parents' car

Then is stopped by the police and injured or killed because of the color of their skin.

We cry.

When a happy LGBTQ+ couple is so excited to get their picture taken on a cruise because they've just married (Finally, thanks to President Obama!)

Then an angry white man encourages his family to sneer, call the couple names, and storms off after making a scene.

We cry.

When a tired Muslim woman wearing her hijab, boards the bus to finally go home after a hard day's work,

Then rude, disrespectful, young men harass her mercilessly because of her belief and hijab, thinking that it is okay to terrorize her.

We cry.

Absolute Truth Will Set Us Free

When parents send their beautiful babies to school, of all different ages from preschool to university,

Then a gunman opens fire with assault weapons and murders their precious babies in cold blood

We cry.

When Trans individuals are finally whom they feel they were born to be and are excited and happy,

Then are abused, abducted, and/or murdered by those who wish to rob them of their life and freedom.

We cry.

When women are mistreated all over America and are denied full civil rights and equality in a free country.

Then men believe that they have complete power over them, dictating what they do with women's bodies, minds, and souls and believe that they also have the right to stalk and kill them should they see fit.

We cry.

When the beautiful little Hispanic child is out playing in the yard,

Then is hit and killed by a stray bullet fired in anger, meant for someone else.

We cry.

When the Indigenous woman sets out in her car just for a peaceful drive,

Then an angry man beats and kills her, hiding her body,

We cry.

When a neuro-diverse child struggles in the public library due to stimuli that has become overwhelming inside the building

Then the librarian bans him/her/they from the library for being "bad"

We cry.

When India doctors or nurses are working in America,

Then patients hate them because of "Hinduphobia".

When a hard-working Asian man is walking down the sidewalk, tired and ready to go home.

Then some angry, racist individual punches him so hard in the face that the poor man falls backwards and dies on the sidewalk from brain damage,

We cry.

When diverse people go out to enjoy the beach, the shopping mall, the amusement park, a restaurant, or anywhere else on this Earth.

Then an angry, ethnocentric racist begins to scream words of hate telling them to go back where they came from or call the police hoping that the police will side with them, the racist.

We cry.

DEAR FRIENDS- Don't you think it's about time we stop *crying* and finally say, *"enough"*? I'd like for you to think about this: Marginalized people altogether, are basically the largest group in America. Did you know that if we all decided to join forces and use our love, gifts, skills, and tolerance for good, we could be a huge and diverse group of action that could peacefully revolt against our country's age-old problem of prejudice and inequality? People don't have to agree with every group's doctrine, belief system, etc., to join and do good! I don't think reasonable people truly want that, anyway! If we were to join politically, we could create one of the largest grassroots organizations in America and peacefully demand full and equal civil rights for all, which would then steer our political system in this country to take care of the *citizens* and not *themselves*. As a uniform front, we could finally rid this country of an old system that is too vile and despicable to even believe, that only serves itself. *The Good Ole Boy System*, which I prefer to call, *the GOBS*. We know the system extremely well in this country, and we've seen the horrendous behaviors, actions, and consequences this system causes. Sadly, it's as old as the United

States. Here is the general definition, *"it is a good ole boy group, club, or system, that is characterized by giving favoritism, power, and special treatment to others because of relational bonds, and is criticized for being corrupt."* You see, people who use this system are very willing to act dishonestly for money, power, and greed. It continues even today and micro-manages our country every day of the year. What I know of the GOBS is that it is a system that wants what it wants immediately and will do anything to get it. That's right, folks, they will do *anything*! Did you just read the part where I said, "our country"? This country is as much ours as anyone else's! We work hard, pay our taxes, and follow the law of the land. If our work and our money are good enough, then *we* are good enough for equality and justice!

The true story that I'm about to tell you is about a brutal, senseless, triple murder, that occurred on New Year's Eve, in 1939, in Oklahoma, where my grandfather is from. Now, folks, understand that I am not an outstanding writer, you'll probably see some mistakes, and that's okay. It's the story that is important here, not my perfect writing skills. In the summer of 2022, I found out that my paternal grandfather had been involved in the above-mentioned crime in some way. It's a story about the good ole boys who were facing dire consequences for their misbehaviors and actions, (or lack thereof), and "fixed" the problem in the GOBS way. The innocent, marginalized people were left to bear the consequences of the GOBS poor choices and self-centeredness.

The Phone Call

I don't even know what date it was, not that it really matters. The thing that matters is the impact that phone call would have on me. I know it was Wednesday, the mid part of June of 2022. My older sister had left a message on my phone telling me that a journalist had been attempting to contact me. She also added that there was something about our Grampa Floyd being involved in a murder. I was immediately irritated because I knew the story very well. I had heard when I was young, that dad's father, my Grampa Floyd, had rustled a cow during the Depression and was put in jail because cattle rustling was a federal crime. That's all I knew so I accepted what I was told. Very simple. You need to understand that I did not know very much about my paternal grandfather back in the day. My dad was very tight lipped about his life, and it was obvious that he had lived a hard and tragic life and had mentioned several times to my sisters and I that he had been raised by his grandparents. He never told us the reason and he really didn't ever discuss the particulars of his overall childhood.

The journalist indeed contacted me on that Wednesday and told me that he was preparing a podcast about America's law enforcement racial injustices in history to present and wanted to talk about my grandfather. Remember, this was the summer of 2022. There had been a lot going on. In March of 2020, we had experienced the trauma and horror of the Covid-19 pandemic, where millions of people died globally of a disease that we had never heard of before. It was horrifying! We all suddenly had to face possible death from a disease that could be spread in so many ways! I remember worrying about even picking up my mail for fear that I could catch this monster of a disease. We had to wear masks and gloves and even quarantine away from other people for a long period of time. Hoarding toilet paper and hand sanitizer became a real thing! Human beings are social animals, and the pandemic did its damage to society in general.

Emotions were running high at the time and suddenly we heard about a black man by the name of George Floyd, who died after a policeman knelt on his neck for approximately 9 minutes and 29 seconds, consequently killing him, during a traffic stop. Three other officers looked on and prevented anyone from interfering with what was happening to Floyd. Protests and riots broke out, feelings were out of control. People began to speak once again of social injustices and inequality.

The journalist who had called me asked some questions about my grandfather, and then asked if I would be willing to read some information that could possibly convince me that my grandfather had been involved in a triple murder in Choctaw County, Oklahoma, on New Year's Eve of 1939. I was dumbfounded, but I was willing to do that.

I was sent news articles about the 1939 crime, and the journalist recommended that I read the book, "Conviction: The Murder Trial That Powered Thurgood Marshall's Fight for Civil Rights", by Denver Nicks and John Nicks, (June 4, 2019). In reading this book I saw my grandfather's name in print for the first time, implicating him in the triple murder with two other convicts, that occurred eighty-four years ago. I could not believe what was happening! Here is the review about the book, and I quote, "On New Year's Eve, 1939, a horrific triple murder occurred in rural Oklahoma. Within a matter of days, investigators identified the killers: convicts on work release who had been at a craps game with one of the victims the night before. As anger at the authorities grew, political pressure mounted to find a scapegoat. The governor's representative settled on a young black farmhand named W.D. Lyons. Lyons was arrested, tortured into signing a confession, and tried for murder. The NAACP's new Legal Defense and Education Fund sent its young chief counsel, Thurgood Marshall, to take part in the trial. The organization desperately needed money, and Marshall was convinced that the Lyons case could be a fundraising boon for both the state and national organizations. He was right. The case went on to the US Supreme Court, and the NAACP raised much-needed money from publicity. Unfortunately, not everything went according to Marshall's plan. Filled with dramatic plot twists, Conviction is the story of the oft-forgotten case that set Marshall and the NAACP on the path that ultimately led to victory in *Brown v. Board of Education* and the accompanying social revolution in the United States." (Amazon Book Review of Conviction.)

I can't even describe just how stunned I was! To add to this incredulous story, the Honorable Thurgood Marshall, (my icon), defended the poor, Black sharecropper who had been framed for the triple murder, and this case had led the way to the victory of *Brown v. Board of Education*? The journalist had gotten my attention! I began to read more and more about Thurgood Marshall and found another interesting read entitled, "The Awakening of Thurgood Marshall-The Case He Didn't Expect to Lose. And Why It Mattered That He Did," written by Gilbert King. I found these memoirs from The Marshall Project, and here is the foreword from "The Awakening of Thurgood Marshall. The case he didn't expect to lose. And why it mattered that he did., was written by Gilbert King. This compilation of memoirs discussed the triple murder case in Hugo, Oklahoma in 1941, and I quote, "*The case that brought Marshall to Hugo, Okla., in 1941, was one of the most extreme. On the evening of Dec. 31, 1939, Mr. and Mrs. Elmer Rogers had been attacked (by ax and shotgun) and killed in their home. Their tenant house was then doused with coal oil and set afire, and 8-year-old James Rogers managed to flee the home, carrying his baby brother, Billie Don, to safety. Four-year-old Elvie Dean Rogers perished in the blaze.*" (The Marshall Project)

It turns out that Thurgood Mashall was deeply impacted by losing the case, *Lyons v Oklahoma,* back in the early 1940s and apparently, from that time on, the Honorable Thurgood Marshall was motivated to strive to protect the rights of all citizens and was hence nicknamed, "Mr. Civil Rights." (Odd thing, I remember reading about Lyons v. Oklahoma many years ago at Montana State University- Western, but it really didn't mean much to me, personally, at that point in time.)

This overload of information blew my mind! I knew my grandfather! I mean, we weren't close but still I knew him, talked with him, hugged him, went to town with him a time or two, went swimming with him, and suddenly I felt extremely angry and very betrayed. I continued searching and found even more news articles about my grandfather being arrested twice for burglary, hence the reason he was placed in the Towsend Prison Camp adjacent to the Rogers family's home in Oklahoma. (It wasn't for killing a cow to feed his poor family, that was for sure!)

Grampa Floyd

My younger sister, Cindy and I have always sarcastically teased each other about our "Carpenter noses". Our noses have a sharp hook, and we always call it our hawk's beak. Our dad had it, grampa had it, and even our great grandfather had it. It's just always been known as the Carpenter nose. I couldn't stand my nose, among other things. I had accidentally broken my nose as a youngster and had a deviated septum. I was so self-conscious about my nose, that when I had surgery done for the deviated septum, as a young adult, I asked my surgeon to please take the hook out of my nose. It was a painful surgery with a long recovery, and I thought it was worth it at the time. Now? I think I should have left it alone. There are always natural consequences to any action. The bridge of my nose is now so thin that it sometimes feels like my nose could fall off at any given moment.

So let me tell you what I remember of my Grampa Floyd. When I was very young, maybe three or four, I remember him bringing a rocking horse over to our house that he had painted. I have no idea where he got it from, but the paint that he used would come off on our hands and clothes when my sisters and I rode the horse. It was silver paint and was most likely lead paint. From what I can remember, he also brought over two ducks named Pat and Mike and they were running around the yard. Funny, I have no idea how long we had the ducks or where they went. Grampa Floyd had the Carpenter nose, of course, very curly hair, and a severed finger and I don't know how he lost his finger. (You know, back then, kids didn't question anything!) Grampa Floyd had met someone and had another family when we all lived in Westwood California, and I don't even know *when* he moved to California from Oklahoma. He had three children who were older than my sisters and me. One time I had heard that Grampa had taken the kids out of school, sold everything, and had gone to Colorado to mine for gold. I don't know if that is fact or fiction. What I do know for a fact is that Grampa Floyd spent a lot of his time dreaming of finding gold and striking it rich! (Funny, I tend to behave in a similar way. I long to go panning for gold and find a huge nugget!)

Another distinct memory that I have is the family getting together in the summer for a picnic at Clear Creek, (just two or so miles from Westwood), and at maybe 4 years old, I was on the bridge watching the fish dart around the pond. I leaned in closely so that I could get a better view of the fish, and suddenly fell headfirst into the pond. It felt like it was in slow motion. I drifted down to the bottom of the pond, all the while seeing the fish darting around in the green water with light beams shining down. My parents, grampa, his wife, and his daughter were sitting on a blanket talking, and apparently, when I fell in, Grampa Floyd began running toward the pond to rescue me, but tripped on a tree root in the ground and apparently broke his toe. My half-aunt got to me first and pulled me out of the water. I can remember this incident just as if it happened yesterday.

In early years, I remember mom and dad playing cards with Grampa and his wife, and occasionally going over to their house. It didn't feel like our family was close to them in my perspective. We never celebrated birthdays, holidays, etc. although I do remember grampa always joking around with my mom saying that when he "struck it rich", he was going to buy her the finest fur coat ever made! A funny thing, I don't ever remember Grampa Floyd working a regular job. After he left Westwood, I remember him occasionally coming to town from the Marysville area, with a very old, large truck filled with peaches or other fruits that he would sell around town, but I do not ever remember him going to a job every day like my dad did. One time grampa brought Johnny Cash's new album to our house and forgot it when he headed back to Marysville. (I may have set it in a place to where he *might* forget it). I played that album so much that I wore it out, but I could sure play the guitar and sing The Ring of Fire!

This is why I felt such shock and horror when I heard about Grampa Floyd's alleged involvement in the 1939 triple murder on New Year's Eve. I mean, I wasn't close to my grandfather by any means, and it didn't seem as though my father was very close with him either, (again just my perspective). But I could not fathom how he could have possibly been involved in such a heinous crime as the one that took place in Hugo, Oklahoma! I just couldn't understand it! I only knew the happy go lucky man, always smiling and cutting up! The guy who was always looking to make a buck and "strike it rich!"

The one thing that I knew beyond a shadow of a doubt, was that my dad had an extremely traumatic childhood, and he did not like to talk about his life in Oklahoma. He wore heavy scars on his back and was extremely stoic and quiet about it. He had talked a few times about running away as a very young child attempting to find his mother, and I did know one thing for sure, he loved his older sister Hazel so much! They had endured all this hell together which I'm sure bonded them strongly. My dad suffered with bouts of depression, high anxiety, a sleep disorder, and stomach problems. He could "loop" on things and imagine the very worst coming to past, traits that I inherited as well.

Folks, this truth that I learned about my grandfather greatly impacted my life in a traumatic way. People have said, "But Dru, it happened 84 years ago, you weren't even born then, so why should it even matter to you?" I'll tell you why. It matters that my blood-related, paternal grandfather was involved in some way, of an awful crime that basically destroyed the Rogers Family and the Lyons Family. I mean, let's face it, it no doubt even impacted Thurgood Marshall's family! I read that Marshall was targeted many times after he represented Mr. Lyons in Hugo, Oklahoma, and even came very close to being lynched at one point in his career, which is so disturbing on many levels! (Tennessee, 1946.)

Back Story

You may ask, "So Dru, who are marginalized people you speak about?" Great question! Marginalized people are those of us who might be diverse in skin color, ethnicity, gender, or culturally. Marginalized populations can be female, people who identify within the LGBTQIA+ community, and people with language or lifestyle differences. Any population who struggles with disabilities, age, neuro diversity etc., can also be marginalized. Any group who is not fully recognized and represented by the government and society is marginalized and take a backseat to the ones in power and do not receive full equality, civil rights, and safety. It may be a woman needing an abortion, a Native American woman trying to get out of an abusive relationship, or a Black man or woman being stopped for a simple traffic violation. It could be a large person being ridiculed and teased or an Asian person walking home from work, an LGBTQIA+ youth going to the mall. And what about the neurodiverse child struggling in a library, or a citizen with mental health difficulties, or a homeless person being teased by a group of the entitled? I mean, let's face it, it can be *anyone* who does not feel represented in our society and who does not feel the full advantage of complete and safe equality. That means that there are countless votes out there that could be used for the good of this country and for all the marginalized people in the country!

You see, if a Book of Life was written about our society, we, the marginalized people, would not be in the book itself, but just placed in the margins as pesky little notes. We are those who have factors that prevent us from reaping all the rights that the main group reaps. It's the homeless who sleep in alleyways, those who struggle in poverty and can't get out, the immigrants who are shunned, the Latino not getting the job, the veteran who has lost everything. I cannot name all the marginalized people, but you all know who you are! Think about it. We're those who are good enough to work hard, pay our taxes to the government *on time,* and should we offend any law of the land, we can be sure that we will pay in a timely fashion. But we're not good enough to be who we are and to feel as though we are validated in society. Many of us do not even feel safe! Think of all the votes that could be used for good! Our differences can prevent us from getting fair and complete equal rights and justice, but together as a large, diverse group of peaceful, good, people, we can be a power to reckon with! We must face the facts that the good ole white boy system, is a system with very deep and ugly roots in American history and it needs to go.

You see, I have been marginalized throughout my entire life. As a kid, I kicked ass in baseball and basketball. I was laughed at when I asked to join Little League. Who had ever heard of such a thing, a girl playing Little League? I played amazingly well, I loved the sport, yet I had to sit on the sidelines due to my gender.

As I grew, I didn't know what my situation was, but I knew that I really didn't "like boys". In fact, I identified very closely with boys and the boys were who I hung out with. In the beginning, I didn't know what I was, but I sure found out when I got a bit older. There were laws against "my kind". Families would disown people "like me", and so I lived an incredibly, sad, and lonely secret, feeling as though I was some kind of evil monster living in a world full of monster slayers. A world of hate, threats, and ridicule, and I truly didn't understand how this could all be "my fault!" I learned quickly that whatever I was, it was bad news, and I could be jailed and even killed for those feelings. At the time, the only knowledge I had about" being gay", was that my cousin was rejected by the family. My dad told me that he had even gone over to my cousin's house and had told him that he needed to get right with God. I now look at my family history and wonder how the secret of my cousin being gay was portrayed as being so much *worse* than my grandfather's involvement in a triple murder situation. *Seriously?* No one wants to be hated in this world. I always dreamed as a kid, of marrying the woman of my dreams. I couldn't. Marriage was forbidden, and so I did what so many other people do and lived the lie with no one knowing. I never confessed to being gay to *anyone* because it was too dangerous. It was a long and lonely life.

I remember when my family went to Oklahoma, I was about 6 years old, and my dad just pulled into a burger place very late at night. When Dad told our relatives where we had eaten, they were mortified! We ate in a diner run by African Americans!

The burgers, shakes, and fries were amazing, and the people were very kind to us! But the family could *not* believe we had made that choice in the 1960s.

In the small town that I was born in, Westwood, California, we had another small little town a mile or two from Westwood, called Pine Town, where many Mexican/Hispanic families resided, and don't think for one minute that many white people were kind when talking about that little town! There was also a residential home for people with disabilities in Westwood, and I remember so many local kids teasing the residents and enjoying it. A few older kids from the place would get extremely dysregulated and would strike out and scream at the kids because the kids were so brutal to them as they took their daily walks. Of course, the parents of those kids doing the bullying would throw a fit because the residents of the place were older, and it didn't seem to bother some parents that their kids were bullying people with disabilities. I had also heard that many people would tell any traveling black people in Susanville, 20 or so miles away, which was a bigger town, that they were welcome to shop and could stop for food, but they'd better not be in the town when the sun went down. (I did not remember seeing any black citizens in this area of California!)

My Life

Please bear with me as I give you my life story, which will then hopefully give you some things to think about regarding many of the troubles that we experience in our world.

I was raised in a quiet little town in Northern California by the name of Westwood, (Lassen County). My father, Drewey Olin Carpenter, originally from Adin, Oklahoma, worked for the lumber company, Collins Pine, in Chester, California. It was 13 miles away from Westwood, and he worked hard and steadily to support his family. I am truly thankful for Dad, providing so well for his family! My mother, Victoria Nadine (Biggs) Carpenter, was a housewife until my adolescent years. I'm also thankful to her for caring for my sisters and me and providing everything that we needed! My Grammas Biggs, (mom's mom) was also a crucial part in my growing up. She would care for us, and would be a huge part of the cooking, tending kids, canning, and preserving foods. Gramma only went to the third grade in school and then had to help at home back in the mid-1900s. Though she only went to third grade, Gramma Biggs became a midwife in Missouri. She told amazing stories about country people and the babies that they produced, with the many things that occurred through her lifetime as an amazing helper in society! My mom was born in Forsythe, Missouri, and traveled with her mother, Idella Marie Collier-Biggs, and her brother, Ronnie Lee Biggs to California. They settled in Westwood after my mother's father, Fred William Biggs, unexpectedly passed away in Missouri, when my mother was only 13 years old. I remember mom's story of hearing her mom scream when she found my grandfather dead after lying down after supper because he reportedly didn't feel well.

An interesting thing regarding immigration. my maternal grandmother, as I mentioned, Gramma Biggs, (Collier), immigrated with her family of 13 children, from Lille, France around 1903 or 1904. I remember her sisters telling us about the family's trip, arriving at Ellis Island, and how the family was horrified to find out that immigration staff had diagnosed my 2-year-old grandmother with a severe case of Conjunctivitis, (Pink Eye), and had quarantined her. Immigration officials warned her parents, that if the eye infection did not clear up within two weeks, she would be sent back to "the old country". I remember my great aunts talking about how horribly frightened they were of being sent back, and possibly being separated. She got well and the family continued their adventures in America.

My grandfather, Fred, served in the U.S. Army during World War I, and was a stone mason by trade, who worked in many areas in Missouri. I remember as a small child, Branson, MO was just land for the most part and homes with no running water, with double outhouses. I am proud of my immigrant family, and I can assure you, that this country is SO much better off because of my maternal family coming to the states! Many of our family have been doctors, lawyers, loggers, teachers, bankers, butchers, steel workers, new reporters, saw millworkers, farmers, business owners, you name it! And hard workers we are! Hurray for the Collier/Biggs Family!

Now think about this. Back when I was a kid, one adult in the family worked, and the other adult stayed home, (if they chose to. I did know women who worked outside the home, and all was great!) The point that I'm getting at is that it was a simpler time back then and even though only one parent worked; my family had what we needed. We had a nice home, two cars, (sometimes maybe older cars, but maintained), we kids had shoes and clothes as well as plenty of winter gear, we had health, dental, and eye insurance through dad's job, and folks, we were able to go on vacation when Dad got his 2-week vacation time *every* August. Christmas, birthdays, and any other holiday/event was taken care of. Think about that! Dad worked in the sawmill, and at the time did not have any higher education! We couldn't even dream of that today! I don't even know how young adults even manage it now! With the prices of rent/mortgage, food, clothing, utilities, gasoline, car payments, and then factor in the health insurance as well as a two week vacation each year? That would be impossible for the average person with no higher education today in 2024! It is taking adults one or two jobs apiece to even come close to what used to be referred to as, "The American Dream."

I have two wonderful sisters, Adele Montgomery, (the oldest), and Cindy Zeluff, (the youngest). My sisters and I attended Fletcher Walker Elementary School, and then later, attended Westwood High School. We all three also attended Lassen Community College in Susanville, CA. My sisters continue to remind me that I was rowdy as a child and got myself into all kinds of predicaments. I once cut a golf ball in two because someone told me that there was a super ball in the center of them, the second I cut the core of the golf ball, it exploded and sprayed some kind of white liquid into my eyes and blinded me for a few days. While playing with my cousins behind the library, I was cutting grass (playing soldiers) and stuck a pocketknife into an artery in my leg. I saw that it was embedded in my leg, I didn't like it there, so I yanked it out. That was a mistake! I even remember at four years old I climbed up on the bathroom sink, got the Bayer Baby Aspirins, put them in my pocket, and teased my younger sister with them telling her they were, "big kid candies and she couldn't have any." I climbed on a chair and stuck my finger into an empty light socket and got blown off the chair. I was in mischief all the time! Many times, my sister took the brunt of it! (Sorry sisters!)

My sisters and I grew up during the Cold War Era, where we practiced Fallout Drills in school, and went to the school gymnasium to receive our various childhood vaccinations, and life seemed simple and ordinary. As kids, we hung out with our cousins and neighborhood friends, rode bikes all over town, we had a Back Alley Gang and we'd play all day, and even spent a great deal of time playing near the train yards on Ash Street. It really was a simpler time. My Gramma Biggs lived close to the trainyard, and we kids would play all day on and near the tracks, making forts, and using the hand trolly, and we stayed very safe. Common sense was abundant and when we headed off to play either Mom or Gramma told us to be careful and move out of the way when we heard the trains coming. We knew exactly what Mom and Gramma said and what they meant, so we spent many summer hours playing and having a great time with our cousins and friends. I mean, life was simple. We could hear the trains coming from over a mile away so we would step off and back away and wait, all the while indicating with our arm and hand going up and down that we wanted the conductor to blow the train whistle! And they did! We spent many summer days swimming in Robber's Creek too! There were so many relatives on my mother's side and neighbors who knew us all so someone always had their eyes on us. Not always for the good, in my opinion. Mom would get phone calls from those who saw me misbehaving quite often!

On my father's side, my dad's father, Floyd Franklin Carpenter Sr., lived a few blocks over from us on Delwood Street, and even though he lived close, we really didn't spend very much time with him. As I've mentioned, I don't know when he came to Westwood, or even California for that matter. As a youngster, I never knew why, but when I asked if we could go over to see Grampa Floyd and our three older, half-aunt and uncles, the answer was usually no. I didn't understand why. It was confusing to me. One time my grandfather invited us to go camping with his family, and I was over the moon with excitement! My father immediately gave an unequivocal, no thank you. I was so upset because I loved camping!

I was an observant kid, and I did notice the adult whispers, especially when we visited my father's sister Hazel, residing in Oklahoma, and when we would visit my father's aunt, whose name was also Hazel, whom my aunt was named after. She lived in the Marysville, California area. There was a lot of talk and whispers. I didn't know what it was all about, but it seemed not okay. My Dad's grandfather, Worry Young Carpenter lived with my Aunt Hazel in California, and we would visit routinely, as my father had been raised by his grandfather and grandmother, Mossie Martha Carpenter. I believe Mossie Martha had passed right after I was born, so I really didn't know her. (The story was that my great grandmother, died when I was 6 weeks old, so dad and mom took me to Oklahoma with them for the funeral. I don't know if Adele went or not, she may have stayed with Gramma Biggs, not sure.) I do remember meeting my paternal grandmother. I think I was about 6 years old, and we had traveled to Oklahoma by car. We visited and stayed with our aunt, uncle, and three cousins in Lawton, OK (I think). When we left their place, we went to another town to see my dad's mother, Elva Thompson Carpenter. I don't remember the name of the city or town where we met her, but we stopped at her house. We three kids sat stone still at her house during the visit, (Please remember that I was very young so exact dates and places are a bit sketchy.) What I noticed about my paternal grandmother, was that she was very slight of build, her hair was somewhat straight, fly away, and gray, and she looked as though her life had been an extremely difficult one for her. She didn't talk much. She seemed to answer dad's questions for the most part, and her answers were short and concise. I mean, dad wasn't much of a talker either, so the visit was awkward. Dad asked if she would like to go to dinner and she said that she thought she could. That was when The Sizzler" was the new up and coming thing. So that's where we went. She got into the back seat of our car with my sister Adele and me, and it seemed very strange. A grandmother that we didn't know, who didn't know us either. Elva was extremely anxious, did not talk to my sister and me, and looked at us like strangers. She would not make eye contact, scooted very close to the backseat door, and would occasionally give my sister and I a very quick and nervous side glance and then would quickly turn away. In my mind, it seemed to me that she was afraid of us. I had heard the adults talking at some point in my life saying that she had suffered greatly from clinical depression and other ailments and had been hospitalized. I never knew the specifics.

What I did know was that dad's family was never talked about. If dad said anything about a family member, it was in very general terms. I did feel that it was somewhat odd that I knew so much about my mom's side of the family, not just my immediate relatives, but all my great aunts, uncles, and cousins, etc., yet didn't know much about dad's family. Dad had great respect for his grandfather, Poppa, and his grandmother, Mossie, as they had raised him for long periods of time. (I was never told why my dad had been raised by his grandparents.) My Dad even brought Poppa back to Westwood for a short visit. By this time, Poppa was in his 80s and was nearly completely blind. In my mind, he was a huge man with distinctive white hair! I remember my mom giving him a shave one morning with a straight razor, something I had never seen before. Poppa had one of those old, old record players, like a gramophone and he played authentic Hank Williams Sr. records on it. They sounded weird to me! By that time, the stereo had been introduced! Also, Poppa challenged my sisters and me to a contest. For every president of the United States that we could memorize and name to him, he would give us a silver dollar for each U.S. President. I know now that these dollars were Morgan Silver Dollars, at the time I had no clue. My sister, Adele, took the challenge, she was the oldest, my sister, Cindy, was probably too young to even be interested, and I couldn't be bothered by memorizing anything! That was too much like school for me! I'd rather do without the dollar! I was a wild tomboy, loved basketball and baseball and I had much more to do than memorizing presidents! I was not the least bit interested! And anyway, if Adele earned the Morgan silver dollars and either saved them, bought clothes, or bought treats like candy, I'd make sure that I would raid her room and get what I needed. Adele and Cindy were always productive. Working, buying clothes, candy, albums, and I would also sneak around, take their stuff, and think that I was a secret agent. Turned out, I wasn't. I took my older sister's "cashmere" sweater one day and thought I was cool and secretive. Turns out someone took pictures at school that day and when the pictures came home, I was in trouble, once again!

Many years went by, and my mother and father suddenly divorced. Mom moved to Utah, taking my little sister, Cindy, with her. Adele was now in college at Chico State University, and I learned to live on my own in Susanville, California, and attended the community college there. It was very difficult for me, but life continued, and eventually, I married, and was absolutely blessed with a set of triplets, delivered at 7 months gestation. I have 2 daughters and 1 son, and their weights were (in order: Madison Elizabeth Earll- 4lbs.4 ounces, Andrew Eugene Earll- 4 lbs.3 ounces, and Stephanie Patricia Earll-Baca-2lbs. 2ounces. My triplets are amazing miracles, and I absolutely love and adore each one of my amazing children! With triplets in my life now, I stayed busy, and life moved very quickly!

Being an average person here in the U.S., with limited resources, I was finally able to get financial aid and attend the University of Montana-Western, in Dillon, MT. We spent 4 years in Dillon, Montana, which was a beautiful place. The kids became teenagers and then headed north and relocated to Havre, Montana, where I taught in Havre, MT, I completed my Master of Education, and then I began to work on my Doctorate. The highline of Montana is incredibly cold! While we were there, it reached 56 below zero at one point! I want to mention that I worked with many Native American, (Indigenous) groups on the "highline" of Montana and was very close to the Rocky Boy Reservation. I immediately realized just how marginalized Indigenous People are in this country! Go visit the reservations and see the beautiful, yet struggling people who continue to be discriminated against and marginalized routinely. The government has done very unfair things against the Indigenous People in America and have marginalized them from the very beginning.

My children graduated and began their own lives, and I met the woman of my dreams whom I had waited for fifty years for. Kim is Canadian, and we got together in 2010. We have been together since then, have moved around quite a bit, traveled, and thankfully, when the amazing President Obama was voted into office, DOMA was struck down, and Kim and I were finally allowed in this country to be legally married in 2014! I will be forever grateful to President Obama for giving Kim and I, the right to marry, as hard working, tax paying, citizens in this country, we should have been given that right so many years ago. And guess what! Hell didn't freeze over, the world did not end, and everyone just continued with their lives. Live and let live. I mean, let's face it, so many progressive countries gave their citizens these rights to marry eons ago!

So, I have now set my story up so that you can hopefully understand a small portion of my life and why I stand here today reminding everyone, SILENCE IS CONDONING and harming us all! Let us not be silenced!

Collecting Information

I spent a lot of time reading and taking notes about the crime that had occurred on New Year's Eve in 1939. The books that I have mentioned gave me a lot of information and gave me ideas of where to turn for more information. I got online and began searching for old records. Ancestry.com has some information, as well as historical records in 'Racine, Wisconsin, etc., but I preferred to work with The Oklahoma Historical Society because there were so many articles and information about the murders and the investigation process, and the people helping me through the Oklahoma Historical Society were amazingly helpful and always kind! They assisted me in finding countless articles and even assisted me in enlarging the old print so that it could be legible for the book. Oklahoma Historical Society, thank you so very much for your assistance and great kindness! They allowed me to use the articles and I am grateful to them!

In looking for various articles regarding the Rogers murders, etc., I read through newspapers dated in the 1940s and saw articles that discussed Hitler, World War Two, Russia, and I even found that the incredibly mundane topics such as food prices, and local news extremely interesting! The prices for cars, farm equipment and food were very entertaining, comparing it to 2024 prices!

I found many articles about the three convicts, (one being my grandfather.) I also found out the truth of how Grampa Floyd got into prison in the first place and those articles are included. It turns out that Grampa didn't "rustle a cow to save his poor starving family", there was plenty of evidence that he had been arrested and convicted of burglary twice and that is how he landed in prison and placed in the Towson Prison Camp in the first place.

I chose to write this book about my grandfather because of several factors. I badly grieved the harm that had been done to innocent people back in 1939 and 1940, which would have lifelong consequences for all of them, and was stunned that Thurgood Marshall, our first Black Supreme Court Justice was involved. But there was another reason. I remembered studying W.D. Lyons v Oklahoma in the 90s as I was at the University of Montana-Western, and it occurred to me that our history books don't necessarily tell the truth about our nation's history. The back story on Lyons v Oklahoma is not accurate. Look how many years we've celebrated Christopher Columbus, when Columbus came to America and was actually a terrorist! We can't forget the religious Native American Boarding Schools where Native American children were taken from their families and literally brutalized with many being murdered! As a nation we simply cannot turn a blind eye to the history of the civil rights movement in this country. One of the central causes of the Civil War was to determine whether slavery would continue and expand westward, thereby creating more states supporting slavery. The Thirteenth Amendment abolished slavery and involuntary servitude. The Fourteenth Amendment addressed citizenship rights and equal protection of the laws for every citizen. The Fifteenth Amendment prohibits discrimination of voting rights. Let me ask you something, did it work? You *know* the answer! In the 1960s we had the Civil Rights Movement and people were murdered once again. Since then, we have continued to fight this battle of discrimination, prejudice, hatefulness for humankind and do you know why? The Good Ole Boy System doesn't like it and continues to change the rules once a law is passed.!

My Grandfather's Involvement in WD Lyons v Oklahoma

Apparently, by the many various documents and articles that I read, my grandfather, Floyd Franklin Carpenter, Sr., along with two other convicts from the prison camp, were accused of the 1939 murder of an innocent family in Oklahoma. Grampa Floyd had been placed in a work camp in an area close to Fort Towson, OK. I will not go into many details about the topographical features of the area, the court documents, etc., because that has already been done. For those who wish to delve deeper into this specific triple murder, in which my grandfather and two other inmates were accused of murder, please read the excellent, and detailed book entitled, "CONVICTION, The Murder Trial That Powered Thurgood Marshall's Fight for Civil Rights", by Denver Nicks and John Nicks. Again, yes, Supreme Court Justice, Thurgood Marshall! I couldn't believe it when I found this out! He has always been such an icon to me and suddenly I felt so sad and ashamed when I realized that this case back in 1939 was one of the cases that Marshall lost. This loss would impact his very life as a black man and attorney, as well as his duties in the Supreme Court. I can't even imagine how he felt about my grandfather back then and isn't it incredible that my grandfather and

Marshall collided into history together! When I read the book, I was stunned! Right there, for all to see, was my paternal grandfather's name along with the other two prison trustees who had been allegedly involved and accused of the cold, calculated, and greedy triple murder. If you would also like to read more about this case, author Gilbert King does a great job of explaining more about this case, W.D. Lyons v Oklahoma, in the book, *"The Awakening of Thurgood Marshall. The case he didn't expect to lose. And why it mattered that he did,"*. Amazingly, during this trial, there were very credible, white people in the courtroom who stated that they knew that the three white convicts had committed the crime and a farmer close to the scene signed an affidavit, swearing that he had seen the three convicts going into the Rogers' home that night in 1939. Even the father of Marie Rogers, (one of the murder victims), joined the NAACP knowing that the local law enforcement had lied on the stand, and many of the white people converged on Attorney Marshall encouraging him and confirming that they knew that the convicts had done it, and that law enforcement were corrupt and lying. Special investigator, Vernon Cheatwood, (The name seems valid), had even admitted to them that he had beaten W.D. Lyons for so many hours that he "hadn't even had time to go to bed". (The Marshall Project.)

Lyons was convicted of a triple murder that he was not guilty of. The memoirs say that the town's people doubled in attendance when Marshall defended Lyons because they were tired of the local government controlling them and pushing them around. They knew that the warden, the police force, and investigators were lying. My grandfather and his two cronies were quickly released, not to be seen or heard from again and they never had to face accountability or responsibility. I just wonder if these accused men involved *ever* thought about that triple murder afterwards. Many years later, when I knew my grandfather, he always showed a happy go lucky, footloose, and fancy-free kind of guy.

I was finally convinced, as I studied newspaper clippings, documents, the book, Conviction, and the memoir, The Awakening of Thurgood Marshall, that the journalist was telling me the truth. The trouble with knowing the truth is, it now means that I must do something about that information. Why, you ask? Well because, even though it had been done in 1939, two innocent families, made of flesh and blood, were destroyed, and I wonder even now, what the history books currently say about this crime. I have a feeling that the lies continue to this very day. This vile act and horrific cover-up of law and court officials used a system that I refer to as "The Good Ole Boy System", (GOBS), to cover up the sloppy, reckless work done by the warden and law enforcement, which really concerned the governor who was concerned about re-election. Once again in this country, GOBS took the poor, powerless, and marginalized people of the time, made them the victims and false perpetrators of this crime and situation, while the ones who were truly "in question" skipped out, leaving their mess for someone else to clean up. GOBS created lies, corruption, and injustice, so that the wrong people were accused, tried, and prosecuted. And that was okay with them if the means met what they wanted the outcome to be. That's horrendous! So, what, right? Who cares? It's been over 84 years! Here's a question for you to answer with your own heart of hearts: Do you think that this kind of corruption is not *still* occurring, even now. in the year 2024? I'll bet, if you're a marginalized citizen, you will agree that it sure does continue to happen. In fact, when I sent my manuscript in for the first time to be edited in April of 2023, I saw on the news that same day, that two law enforcement officers were angry at two black reporters in Oklahoma and were overheard to say that it was "too bad that lynching wasn't still legal in the U.S." Can you hear me!? This system *continues* and *must* be eliminated from the face of the earth, if we wish for all human beings to have equality, equity, and quality of life!

Okay, so now I will go through the entire story with you. It's brutal and it crushes me every time I read, think, or write about this crime. I think of my grandfather whom I knew as an easy going, "no worries" kind of guy, and I wonder how just how, the obsessive greed could have taken over to the point where human lives did not matter. Remember, I can only speculate because Grampa and his other 2 friends were conveniently and quickly released in a streamlined way to protect the warden, law enforcement, and the governor. The law enforcement officers were apparently willing to lie and manipulate the system to protect their bosses. My grandfather and his cohorts were accused of the murders, and testimony revealed that the three men had been planning, while in the brothel, drinking, to get their money back from Mr. Rogers. During the trial, again, an upstanding, farmer, in court, testified and signed an affidavit stating that he did indeed witness my grandfather and his two trustee friends going into the Roger's house on that New Year's Eve night on the day and time in question. This burns into my very soul. I feel that I, as a blood relative, must speak the absolute truth. I won't know for sure because of the cover-up. But in case these three convicts were indeed guilty, I send my heartfelt sorrow to those who were victimized and destroyed in the name of money, greed, and corruption. It certainly shows that the Good Ole Boy System, the system thriving and reeking for centuries in this country, was once again at play at the time the murders occurred. And just as present day, the GOBS back then was caked with lies, excuses, greed, power, and soaking in a brine of hateful ethnocentricity. If people did not think that they were so superior to all other flesh and blood human beings, crimes like this would not happen. *May this ABSOLUTE truth set us ALL free,* and hopefully inspire us in the year 2024, to become motivated to overcome the hatred and crimes of others, so that we, the chronically oppressed, marginalized people of the country and the world, may become empowered, knowledgeable, and proactive advocates in the name of civil rights for all! Become powerhouses in your world! We must refuse to continue to be the oppressed people of America and insist on truth, justice, equality, and civil rights for all! We have worked hard, we have followed the law of the land, and we pay our taxes, therefore, we shall *peacefully* seek every right available in this country!

The Murders

As I've mentioned, Grampa Floyd was apparently in a prison work camp, adjacent to the town of Hugo, OK, according to the authors, Nicks, D. and Nicks, J., and we must remember in history that Oklahoma had been hit with extreme disasters at the time like The Dust Bowl and the Depression Era. Did you know that during the 1930s this phenomenon called The Dust Bowl, killed so many people and animals, it caused over two and a half million human beings to flee from areas of Texas, New Mexico, Colorado, Nebraska, Kansas, and Oklahoma? Farmers' soil basically blew away due to unsound farming practices. This was also after World War I and apparently, Oklahoma had not even recovered yet from that, so countless Oklahomans headed to other places, with many heading for California, (As a kid, I had to read John Steinbeck's book, The Grapes of Wrath.) This is indeed the story of what was happening to Oklahomans during this time era. Humans, animals, and farms were destroyed. People were desperate to make a living on lands where growing any crop became impossible, causing them to flee Oklahoma during this horrific and damaging time, with many people having nothing but the worn out, threadbare clothes on their backs. Let's also remember that The Great Depression had also occurred in this country from 1929 through 1939. Times were extremely brutal and harsh during these times, and mass people suffered. Oklahomans in the day, had suffered greatly. At the beginning of the state's birth in 1907, racism was going strong, and one of the first two laws to pass after statehood was to ban interracial marriage and ban interracial schools. No big surprise there, right? You see, back in those times, people who were not white, lived under the racist legal codes *and* laws of the land. Jim Crow Laws were basically set up to say to the world, hey, we're separate but equal, and yet the system was not equal and prevented anyone of color from achieving and obtaining equitable rights and treatment. Black Americans were not allowed to vote, were paid significantly less than white Americans, and black students could be banned from attending higher education of any kind.

So, here's the incredibly sad story of some Oklahomans who had more than their fair share of trouble, and then, things got worse. It is incredibly sad, vicious, with such greedy undertones and the question that I keep asking in my head is, *was ninety dollars truly worth the cost of destroying so many people's lives over?*

There was an old rickety farmhouse in the middle of a large field near Ft. Towson. A poor, white sharecropper, and his wife and three small children lived in this old house. These people were so poor that they didn't even have the simplest of luxuries like curtains, or even enough chairs for their little family of five to sit on. Readers, this is awful, and I apologize for having to be so graphic about what happened. I will list their names first. I must because they need to be honored! As I write this, I take breaks because it is so awful and brutal that it tears my heart apart! Please hear their names and honor them, yes, even though it's been over 84 years ago, let's please honor them all! Elmer Rogers, born in 1909 in Oklahoma and died, December 31, 1939, buried in Fort Towson Cemetery. He was thirty years old. Anna Marie Colclasure Rogers, born 1911, died on December 31, 1939, buried in the Fort Towson Cemetery, she was twenty-eight years old. Elvie Dean Rogers, born in 1935, died on December 31, 1939, buried in the Fort Towson Cemetery, and he was four years old. The surviving brothers: (the oldest son), James Glen Rogers, 1932-1987, and (the baby), Billy Don Rogers, 1938-1994.

I also wish to mention W.D. Lyons family as well. I have not been able to find anything about his family at all. Let's remember that he had to leave his family when he was sent to prison for a crime that he did not commit. Lyons was released in 1961 and blended back into society, but I know nothing about how this man was after his prison time. Did he re-join his family? Were they okay? Even though I don't know their names, I wish to honor the Lyons Family as well. And isn't it fitting? I can find everything I need for the white folks. Did anyone care about the black family whose life was destroyed as well?

Elmer Rogers, the poor, white sharecropper, with his wife, Marie Rogers, were raising three beautiful sons. James Glen Rogers, 7 years old; Elvie Dean Rogers, 4 years old, and the baby, Billie Don Rogers, 1 year old. It was bedtime on that New

Year's Eve in 1939, when murderers shot through a window with a shotgun, which immediately disabled Elmer who was shot in the ribs with buckshot, and was found lying between two beds, soaked in his own blood, glass shards scattered around, and his skull crushed. Elmer's wife, Marie, was found dead on their porch, shot in the torso, and found lying in her own blood along with her own crushed jaw and brains around her. You see, not only was a shotgun used on them, but the murderers also used an axe, (most likely picked up right in the Roger's own yard)

Readers, I am so very sorry that I must be descriptive, but this was the crime scene. Again, it takes time for me to write this because I become so saddened and overwhelmed by the sheer brutality of this crime and realize that the murders occurred over ninety dollars from a gambling game!

Apparently, when the intruders shot Elmer through the window with buckshot, Marie screamed at their oldest son, James, to grab the boys and run. It was bedtime and the kids were in their beds. I read that Elvie was most likely asleep in his bed when poor little James was told by his dying mother to grab the boys and run, and that's what he tried to do. James dragged his baby brother out of the house as the house was being burned down. The poor little guy had to have been terrified beyond belief! James continued to say later, that he had seen 2 men come into the house, he didn't know if they were black or white, but he thought that they had black leather gloves on. James ran quite a way to the highway with the one-year-old baby and was found by a passerby, exhausted and in shock. The two little boys were extremely cold, and James was hysterically trying to tell adults what had happened to his poor family. Law enforcement was notified, and the investigation began.

Now apparently, these big bad men who cowardly shot through a poor man's window at bedtime, killed the man and woman, with buck shot, and then had hacked on them with a double-edged ax. They then went back outside, poured coal oil around the house, and set the house on fire to cover up the crimes. Little James ran through the dark, like the hero that he was, carrying his baby brother, Billie, heading for the road. I can't even imagine what James's thoughts were as he was running for his very life, after seeing his parents murdered and maimed, and then having to also leave his little brother, Elvie, behind because he didn't know where he was. The little 4-year-old, Elvie Dean Rogers, had been in his bed, very possibly asleep at the time of the crime, and then most likely awakened to the horrendous noises, screaming, and chaos, and had gone under his bed. (In some of the stories about this incident it does say that Elvie was under his bed.) You must understand that this was a grisly murder and a very huge happening at that time near Hugo, Oklahoma, and newspapers from all over the U.S. were reporting about it.

After the murders, the talk and gossip was like wildfire. Apparently, there were a lot of tips coming in from people who knew who had done it. Word of mouth was that there had been a dice game on December 30, 1939, that had occurred at a person's "house", that also doubled as a brothel, and three convict trustees were there playing dice, and Elmer Rogers had won the game, winning ninety dollars. There was strong talk that the three convicts were the ones who had murdered the Rogers Family because of the ninety dollars that they had lost in the game. When law enforcement found out about the house being burned down, they immediately questioned the convict named Lambert, who was friends with the other two convicts. Incidentally, this "suspect" had very singed hair, imagine that! Lambert confessed, saying that he had driven the car and Wellmon as well as Carpenter had been involved. All three of these men had been prison "trustees" at the prison camp. A white, well-known farmer in the community, said that he had witnessed the three prison trustees, (one identified as my Grampa Floyd), entering the Rogers' family house on the evening of New Year's Eve in 1939. He was positive, swore an oath, and signed an affidavit claiming that he had seen the convicts go into the house.

Lambert said he didn't participate in the murders, the other two convicts "made" him drive the car and threatened to kill him if he drove away. The prison trustees suddenly all said that they didn't do it. (Hmm, I wonder where the singed hair came from.)

Evidence and word leaned strongly towards that thought that the three convicts had indeed murdered Mr. and Mrs. Rogers and their little 4-year-old son, Elvie. Can you just imagine how James went through life, witnessing his mother and father being shot with buckshot and their skulls being crushed in by an ax, along with living through the part where he, as a small child, left his little 4-year-old brother, Elvie, who burned to death in the fire? An interesting thing that I just found out. James died in 1987 at fifty-five years old, in Texas. The baby, Billy Don, died in 1994, in Texas as well, and he was fifty-five years old! I thought that was a strange thing, both dying at fifty-five years old.

I just couldn't figure out why my grandfather and the other convicts were released immediately. They weren't really that *"special"* per se, in the scheme of things, that would cause the prison system to simply release all three of them immediately and find Lyons as the scapegoat. I mean, they didn't have clout, power over the system, or anything else that I could imagine. But then I realized, the warden was not doing his job was he? He allowed these convicts to come and leave Fort Towson Prison Camp as "trustees", at will, and were allowed unsupervised hunting with shotguns, hanging out with the locals, and were even allowed to gamble and drink in town, hanging out at the local brothel, (which, again, apparently doubled as a house). I could then see it. It really had nothing to do with the three convicts being extraordinary, it had everything to do with the GOBS in power once again!

Things weren't looking very good for the Good Ole Boys, Warden, Jess Dunn and the Governor, Leon Chase Phillips. They realized that this sloppy work could be extremely damaging to their reputations and the murders would cause an enormous political scandal. So, what did they do? *THEY RELEASED THE CONVICTS WHO CREATED THIS ENTIRE PROBLEM.* And that fixed it how? I'd love to know what the three prison camp trustees did immediately after they got out. Again, there are time frames that leave me wondering, such as: Could this have been why my father's mother had gone into a treatment facility? I mean, who wouldn't if their spouse had been involved in such an awful crime? There were stories of my father having to be raised by his grandfather and grandmother, and, I mean, the time frame seems to fit. My dad told us that he had to be raised by his Poppa Carpenter and that he was around five or six years old and had run away from Poppa's to try to find his mother, who was in a different town. Hmmm…My dad was born around 1933, and the crime occurred in 1939. I know, there are no hard facts around that, but it sure makes me wonder.

So now, with the three convicts released early, law enforcement found an innocent, black scapegoat. William Douglas Lyons, a marginalized human being, to be framed for the murders, who was beaten and tortured into making a confession. Willie D. Lyons, a 21-year-old, poor, husband and father, was a black sharecropper. He had been out hunting rabbits with a borrowed gun and had been celebrating the New Year, I guess at his mother-in-law's house, by apparently stepping outside occasionally for a nip of moonshine.

It's interesting that the release of the three convicts aligned with the arrival of the governor's special investigator, Vernon Cheatwood. (I laugh every time I say his name! It seems very fitting!) How convenient for the GOBS of the time! Suddenly, Lambert who had confessed and named himself and the other two convicts in the beginning, (you know, the guy with the "noticeably" singed hair), then conveniently changed his story and said that the perpetrator was a black man by the name of William Douglas Lyons. (Of course, he would!) I can see why Thurgood Marshall was haunted by this case. So am I. The case was a rigged deal from the very start, all because the GOBS were sloppy, and they knew they were in trouble if the truth came out so they covered their own asses so that they could continue being in power. So, basically, the convicts were not special, it was simply the fact that if the convicts were accused, tried, and sentenced for the murders, it would have been revealed that the warden and governor were sloppy and inept, and they would have lost their jobs. And let's remember, GOBS always does what it wants and gets what it wants no matter the cost!

Well, low and behold, the warden of the Towson Prison Camp, Jess Dunn, could see that his ass was on the line now, and so he immediately shut down the prison camp, and promptly sent all the convicts to the state penitentiary in McAlester, Oklahoma. Of course, a lower employee, a camp sergeant, became the scapegoat and was fired after the news that the convicts in question had confessed to the murders because Elmer had beaten them in a dice game, and they went out there to "retrieve" their money. (I hope that you can feel the disgust and horror of this situation as I do! Ninety dollars.)

I still don't understand it. Over 84 years ago, racist white men in very high places, covered up a vile and senseless crime all because they wanted to keep their jobs, and remain in power. Does this sound familiar? Nothing has changed in 84 years! Why does this horrible cycle continue? WHY? Think about it! Are we truly doing enough to get rid of the corrupt Good Ole Boy System that continues to assault, intimidate, and threaten, the marginalized and oppressed populations? You know the answer just as I do. Absolute truth could set us free from this menace!

The Trial

And now I will tell you about the "Kangaroo" court trial. (I mean no disrespect to the poor kangaroos of the world.) I want to be very clear so I will define a kangaroo court from the internet: *"It's a mock court where the principles of justice and law are corrupted without regard."* Well, there you go! This was exactly what happened! Let's remember that the three convicts from the prison camp were immediately released, coinciding with the arrival of special investigator, Vernon Cheatwood. And please, I encourage any of you who are interested in this kind of injustice, to do some checking around and read about cases like these. I mean, this case is not the only case in which blatant injustice has occurred or is occurring! Check out The Marshall Project Nonprofit Journalism about Criminal Justice, and The Oklahoma Bar Association Bar Journalism, etc. The information is out there, people just need to get a spark of interest and begin reading! Remember, knowing about these injustices is half the battle! It's easy to turn a blind eye, convince ourselves that there's nothing we can do. But there is! Reject apathy!

So, back to the trial, and I got a lot of this information from the Oklahoma Bar Association as well as the other references listed. A civil rights activist in Oklahoma, named Roscoe Dunjee had apparently called the Harlem, New York Office of the NAACP, telling them of an Oklahoman who had been tortured into a false confession of a triple murder. Young Thurgood Marshall, at the time, oversaw the legal division but was only making a paltry salary so he was also delivering groceries to supplement his income. He agreed to go to Hugo, Oklahoma to defend William Douglas Lyons, the young black man who was charged with the violent crime.

The facts during the trial showed that Lyons had been tortured into confessing to the horrific crime. Poor Lyons had been transported to the County Prosecutor's Office and during transport, had been repeatedly beaten in route, and then was beaten again for hours, once they arrived, by Vernon Cheatwood and the County Sheriff. Mr. Lyons was threatened with red hot irons if he did not confess and then one of the most heinous behaviors imaginable occurred. Cheatwood and the Sheriff placed a pan on Lyon's lap, holding some of the charred remains of little Elvie Dean's little body! Mr. Lyons finally signed the confession at 2:30 a.m. because he could not stand the cruel abuse anymore! Of course, when Vernon Cheatwood was asked in court if he had ever been abusive to Lyons, Cheatwood swore that he had not. Thurgood Marshall called a bookkeeper from the local inn to the stand and asked her if Cheatwood had asked her to "forget" about his request that she help him find his blackjack so that he could show it off to the other guests at the inn. She said that yes, he did, and that she refused to "forget it" because it would be a lie.

The prosecutor, by the name of Horton, (you know, the one who helped Cheatwood beat Lyons into submission and placed the charred remains of a little boy's body on his lap), was grilling Lyons about his testimony that people had tortured him and reminded him that the numerous people who had sworn that Lyons had *not* been tortured were "good, upstanding citizens and officers of the court". Lyons replied to the prosecutor, saying that Horton should know the truth about what happened because he was right there participating in beating him with the rest of them. The prosecutor got flustered, and after denying Lyon's statement, and people laughed loudly in the courtroom, Horton then made the excuse that he had only been there, trying to stop the officers from beating Lyons, and the crowd laughed loudly again. Sheriff Harmon was called to the stand. Lyons further alleged that he had been fastened to the wrist of a deputy and beaten and placed in the room where the electric chair was and was kept there until he once again signed a confession and affidavit swearing that no force had been subjected upon him by anyone. In several of the references that I read, Thurgood Marshall had mentioned that he sure enjoyed the fact that by the mid part of the trial, all the black population and 90 percent of the white people in the courtroom sided with W.D. Lyons and knew that he was not guilty. Marshall said that it gave those people who had always been pushed around by such a racist system, a chance to laugh and to see the racists officers be shown for who they truly were in court. Regardless of all the evidence that proved that W.D. Lyons was not guilty of the triple murders, the jury still found him guilty and of course when the case was appealed Lyons lost again. Thurgood Marshall stayed in touch with Douglas Lyons and often paid for things that he needed in prison. In 1961 Lyons was released from prison.

Parallels Between 1939 and 2024

So, the first question that I want to ask you is this: do you see any similarities between the triple murder coverup that occurred back in the 1940s, and today's ridiculousness in the U.S.? Just read the news and you'll see! Things really haven't changed that much. Why? After 84 years, things should have significantly changed and yet, are all human beings equal in 2024? No. Do you have a strong government *for the people*? No, the people in government are basically concerned about themselves, their own self-interest, and the profits that power and influence brings. You know, our Founding Fathers, back in the day, spoke about the need for rotation in office because they were so concerned that not doing so would cause corruption, abuse of power, and a permanent political class. This is exactly what has happened to our government. Our politicians have become professional politicians and are completely out of touch with the average American citizen! I agree with our Founding Fathers, politicians should serve for a limited time and then go right back to their private lives. It would certainly save the country from a lot of corruption, power mongers, and greed! (See, Professor, I *was* listening in my American History class in Dillon, Montana! It was an awesome class by the way!)

I'm afraid that we are going to need new parties in our political system. We've got to have a system that takes care of all of us, and a system that is not so hateful towards the other party. We need gun control. Legal adults owning legal firearms have got to understand common sense. Lock up your guns and don't make them available to children, adolescents, and irresponsible adults! There were six hundred thirty mass shootings in the United States in 2023, and by January 15, 2024, there have been *five mass shootings so far*. Does anyone see a problem with this? Our kids go to school and must go through ALICE Training for active shooters in our schools. Repeatedly, we have mass shootings in this country and repeatedly the gun owners scream about their own rights. Common sense, my friends, just plain and simple, common sense! I hear all about the gun owners' rights to carry guns, but don't you think that the precious children in our country should have the right to live and to be safe in their schools and home environments? Children are our future! We spend way too much time playing with rhetoric while countless human beings die from guns and mass shootings. Common sense!

And let me ask you this: Are you able to work and live comfortably without every adult member having to work multiple jobs just to keep a roof over your heads and food on your tables? I don't know how young adults do it now! If you can *find* a place to rent, the rent is outrageous and people must come up with first, last month's rent, cleaning deposit, pet deposit, and it costs thousands! The last time Kim and I rented, it cost us upwards of three thousand dollars. Just to rent a house! If you don't get paid a decent wage, how can you pay thousands to get into a rental or a mortgage? These are all the questions that we must ask ourselves as we move forward. I have been homeless and jobless. I've washed clothes in a bathtub, (jeans were brutal to wash by hand!) Does the government take care of our needs? They do not! Do you get a baby/child bonus each month to help you out in this high-priced world where there is no consideration for families raising children? Nope! And let me ask you, does the country concern itself with citizen's health and welfare? That's a hard no, especially if you've tried to buy health, eye, dental, or prescription insurance! If folks do get health insurance at an astronomic price, what does it cover? Many times, we spend so much on insurance yet still have high medical bills that build up because of copays, deductibles, etc., and then we're threatened by the hospitals and other businesses demanding money! It doesn't make any sense! (Hmm, maybe we should also talk about Big Pharma where it costs an arm and a leg to get even the basics like insulin, Epi Pens, and a host of other lifesaving medications! Yes, you heard me Big Pharma, don't act so innocent!)

Does our government help us with waste management, or more efficient energy and ways to save our poor old Earth from human destruction? Are you able to get an education for higher learning so that hopefully, you can improve life for yourself and your family? But then, if you do get a higher education, what do you do about the student loans? How can you pay student loans back when job wages are not commensurate with the amount that we must pay back in loans? And why should we have to pay anyway? Isn't it for the betterment of our country if we do become educated and move forward? I'm telling you; our government sets us up for failure each and every day!

What about abortion? Do you know that I graduated in 1973, the year that Roe v. Wade won a landmark decision? Fifty years later, Roe v. Wade is overturned. Can you hear me? *Fifty years later?* This is exactly what I'm talking about. Back to the Dark Ages once again! Just like our Civil Rights. We get a little ahead in this country and then the GOBS does its "magic" and reverses all the things that we believe will help us as human beings! We never get ahead, and we will never progress as a country with the GOBS! This country is a melting pot of diverse people now with many cultures, lifestyles, and beliefs. And when we are hated by those who *claim* to be righteous, just remember, if they *were* righteous, they wouldn't be haters, (*because you will know them by their fruit*). The marginalized people of the country must stand up, band together, and peacefully declare that it is time to get what we need! Just remember, systems like the GOBS want one thing: Power and control over us! That's how it works. But we can say *"that's a hard nope"!*

So, you see, the GOBS still do what they want no matter the cost, diverse people are still the scapegoats, and hatred runs rampant. Lies continue and people follow them hook, line, and sinker, such as eating horse worm medicine to cure Covid, declaring that the moon landing never happened, and pushing the ridiculous agenda that the world is flat. (I read an article that said an estimated hundred thousand people may have died by taking that ridiculous horse worm medicine instead of getting proper treatment for Covid.)

You see, the truth *was* in the courtroom when W. D. stood trial for the Rogers' murders, that he did not commit. And yet, even with ample evidence revealing that he did not murder those people, the jury followed the GOBS and found him guilty anyway because that's what the GOBS wanted. I'm sure the governor and warden then went on their way, (along with many of the participating law enforcement officers), doing exactly what they wanted: which was reaping the money and use power once again to control the masses.

The pain is real, you know. Fellow human beings were hurt all over this country when the policeman recklessly knelt on George Floyd's neck for *9 minutes and 29 seconds*, which corrects the 8 minutes 46 seconds timing that was originally thought. Breonna Taylor was needlessly shot down, the gifted 16-year-old kid, Ralph Paul Yarl who went to pick his sister up and mistakenly went to the wrong door, was shot to death, and then what about Christian Hall, Melissa Ventura, or Mario Gonzalez? I can just imagine as you read this, that *you* can think of human beings who should be honored and remembered because they were sadly sacrificed by the haters of the world. Marginalized, living, breathing human beings in our country are cut down because of the lack of tolerance and prejudice. Make no mistake about it, there is no place in our society for the Good Ole Boy System anymore. It should have never been here in the first place, and I'll tell you why. Because when they do what they want to do to preserve their own lust for power and greed, they are walking on the backs of every marginalized person in the United States!

Did My Dad Know?

Before I close this story up, there is something that I have been thinking about for two years now, and really don't know what to do with it. (This information did not register with me or even make sense for years and is possibly nothing at all). Firstly, do I know 100% that my father knew of the crimes that his father had been accused of committing? I do *not* know that for certain because no one ever said anything in my family. I think he did, and I think that it caused him a lot of emotional pain. My father feared the police and always taught us to obey the law, plus, he never really wanted to be involved in any controversy whatso*ever*! Dad passed away in the summer of 2010. His beautiful and loving wife, Barbara, whom my children and I loved and adored, survived him. You see, Gramma Barbara lived for several years longer, and I don't remember the date that she died, but she passed somewhere around 2015 or 16, not sure. But there is a reason that I mention this. Dad was an unusual man; and had some odd behaviors that sometimes would make us kids laugh and shake our heads. I remember when I was very young; my family went to British Columbia in a rented travel trailer. He had his trusty .22 rifle with scope packed in the trailer that we vacationed in. When we got closer to the Canadian Border, he pulled over, drove on a dirt road, got a shovel out, and proceeded to bury his rifle because he certainly couldn't take it over the Canadian border. When we came back, he took that same little dirt road, stopped at that specific spot, and dug it up, then we went along our merry way. One of my daughters told me at one time, that she had seen this unexpected behavior when Poppa and Gramma took the kids camping. He buried a gun for some reason, and then he later dug it up, and again, went along his merry way.

After my stepmother died, her daughter sent me something very unexpected. A treasure map, and there were also a few pictures included. The pictures were of some guns. I didn't know what it was all about and had never known my dad owned these guns. When I got the map and pictures, I thought it was a little strange but, my dad had some funny quirks, so I just packed them all away for keepsakes, thinking that there was no way at the time that I could even afford to travel to California and then knew I couldn't just dig anywhere that I apparently needed to dig.

Upon learning about my grandfather's story in Oklahoma in the 1940s, I quickly searched for that map and those pictures. Understand me, I do NOT even know for sure about the pictures, but I do know that dad wanted me to see that map. The pictures are of about 6 or so guns. I know about guns, and I noticed that there was a very old 12 gauge shot gun and it looked like an old .410 shotgun. The others don't appear to be as old. After I looked at the pictures again, I remembered that the journalist who originally called me had told me that the "murder weapon" had never been found, Apparently, investigators had found the axe, which had been burned in the fire at Rogers' home.

I can't help but wonder. Had my father's dad, my grandfather, talked him into hiding something for him? (I mean, dad was only 5 or so when the crimes took place.) But in looking back, my grandfather was a con man through and through. He was always looking for a "get rich scheme", going to mine gold for the big payoff and most of his visits would center around how he could make it rich by the scheme of the day, and he was always trying to get others to join him in whatever scheme he had for the moment. Could Grampa Floyd have asked my dad at some point in his life to hide or bury something for him? I find it very odd that I was sent a treasure map, *after* my stepmother died. (By the way, I *knew* the map was from dad because he had very distinct and odd penmanship, and I also noted that the "treasure" had been moved three times before I received the map for whatever reason.)   Did dad bury guns for his father? I mean, what if? I know about guns in general, and I saw the pictures. Two shotguns are very old, one, I thought that the .12 gauge looked like a Winchester model 1897, but I'm not 100% sure, I didn't recognize anything about the .410 except that it was old. I wonder and ponder about it, (mind you, it's been over 84 years later).

I mean, I cannot just simply drive to a small town in the country and start digging and hunting for treasure on public land 84 years after the fact. Things would have greatly changed. For a fleeting second, though, I had thought about going and attempting to find that treasure. But here's my fascination: You see, the weapon was never found, over 84 years ago, when the Rogers Family was murdered on New Year's Eve in 1939.

Sometimes I just wonder, what if my dad wanted this horrific secret to come out so that all would know? Is that what the map was about? After I had found the gun pictures, I contacted the journalist who had first informed me about my grandfather's involvement in the case that occurred so long ago, so I asked him if the murder weapon had been a .12 gauge or a .410 because both guns look very old. His response shook me to the core because his reply was, "Dru, I didn't mention it before, but there were 2 shotguns…"

Closing Chapter

In closing, thank you so much for reading my book. I felt that I had to speak out about what I had learned because that incident long ago, impacted so many people, and the system that protected "the wrong people" during the crime in 1939, is the very same system that *continues* to protect the wrong people in present day America.

We all have choices to make. So many people are unequally treated, and I just want to say that you have done an amazing job trying to "hang in there", in a system that keeps so many of us struggling. Just please remember, if the *marginalized people* would agree to join forces in a tolerant, kind, and peaceful way, our voting booths during elections could erase away forever, the Good Ole Boy System, (again the GOBS), with their archaic, judgmental beliefs, their hateful rhetoric and their ugly racism. We could do it!

I still hear one song occasionally that was recorded back in the early 1970s called One Tin Soldier? It was written by Dennis Lambert and Brian Potter and was first recorded in 1969. As a kid I would listen to it, and always wondered WHY the Valley People were so dang greedy that they refused to share the riches that the Mountain People had offered them? Why couldn't they just join the Mountain People, do what we've all been taught in school, which is: play fairly, clean up after yourself, always be kind, share with others, and everyone could live in peace, harmoniously? The Valley People were too greedy and ethnocentric! They must have thought that *they* were the supreme beings, that no other humans mattered, and made sure to get rid of anyone who was even remotely known as a Mountain Person. *They didn't want to share you see, they wanted it all and it wasn't even their riches!* The Mountain People had the treasure, they wanted to share it with them, and yet, the Valley People just had to mount their horses, draw their swords, bust up the mountain, and viciously, and brutally slaughter ALL the Mountain People so that they could greedily reap the entire treasure for their own. Finally, after slaughtering every mountain being there was, they hustled on over to the treasure that had been buried beneath a rock, and they greedily lift out that rock and realize, that the treasure that the Mountain People kept so sacredly hidden and cherished was simply the basic notion of how important *Peace on Earth* truly was and is. *PEACE* was the Mountain People's greatest treasure of all. How very tragic and sad for humankind, how very sad indeed...Let's fix *our* countries situation!!

I think this book would make a wonderful movie for such a dynamic, heroic man as the Honorable Thurgood Marshall! Let's remember all the selfless, caring, and loving human beings who sacrificed and those who continue to sacrifice so much to fight for Civil Rights for All!

Hopefully, my next books with be a series of children's behavioral books that can teach and entertain children but will have handy strategies and hacks for families that can hopefully make life much easier when dealing with children with emotional and behavioral deficits, *(my actual professional forte)*. Ser Oliver Newton and Lady Kya Kitten, Kim and my little Yorkies, will be the hero/heroine in these books!

My friends, please be safe, strong, and kind out there! Keep a song in your heart and *know* that you are an amazing and wonderful human being, and we've got this! Happy Trails! dru

References

Davis, Michael. (May 2023.) Injustice in Choctaw County: How a Largely Forgotten Oklahoma Trial Set Thurgood Marshall On a Path to Power. Oklahoma Bar Association. Retrieved from www.//ok.bar.org/barjournal/may-23/injustice-in-choctaw-county-how-a-largely-forgotten-oklahoma-trial-set-thurgood-marshall-on-a-path-to-power

Gilbert King. (November 20, 2014.) The Awakening of Thurgood Marshall: The Case He Didn't Expect to Lose and Why it Mattered That He Did. The Marshall Project: Nonprofit Journalism About Criminal Justice. Retrieved from https://www.themarshallproject.org

Nicks, Denver, & Nicks, John. (June 4, 2019). Conviction: The Murder Trial That Powered Thurgood Marshall's Fight For Civil Rights.

King, Gilbert. (November 20, 2014.) The Awakening of Thurgood Marshall: The Case He Didn't Expect to Lose and Why it Mattered That He Did. The Marshall Progject: Nonprofit Journalism About Criminal Justice. Retrieved from https://www.themarshallproject.org

Lambert, Dennis, & Potter, Brian. (1969.) Song: One Tin Soldier

Oklahoma Historical and Research Center. Oklahoma City, OK. www.okhistory.org

Wikipedia. (2024.) Retrieved at https://www.en.wikipedia.org

About the Author

DruAnne Carpenter-Earll was born in Westwood, California, and hold both a graduate and a postgraduate degree in education. She grew up raising Scottish Highlanders in the Sierra Nevada Mountains, where she came to know scorpions, horny toads, and rattlesnakes. As a gay woman with Asperger's Syndrome, she is passionate about reaching neurodivergent people, the LGBTQ+ community, and anyone else who feels marginalized by society. With a fruitful life spent on both U.S. coasts and almost everywhere in between, DruAnne plays twelve-string guitar, sings, fishes, and paints. She considers herself hysterically funny and promises to never grow up.

www.ingramcontent.com/pod-product-compliance
Lightning Source LLC
LaVergne TN
LVHW020419070526
838199LV00055B/3666